DOODLE BOOK

Doodle Fun Made Easy

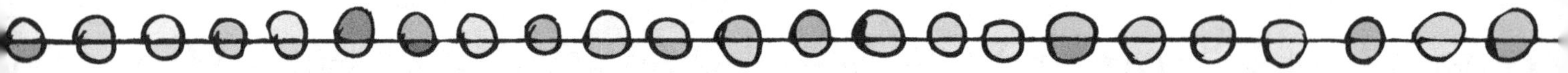

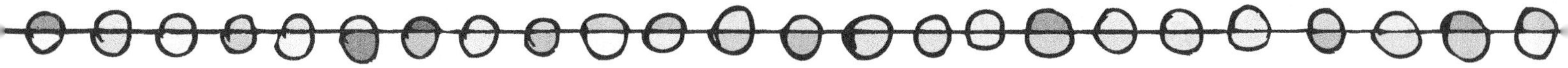

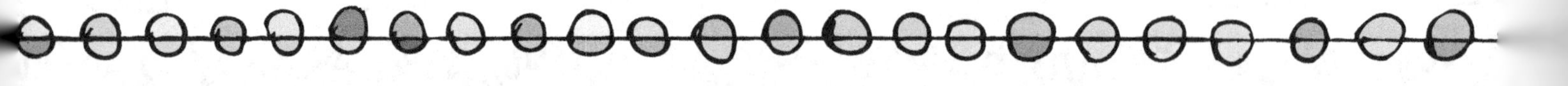

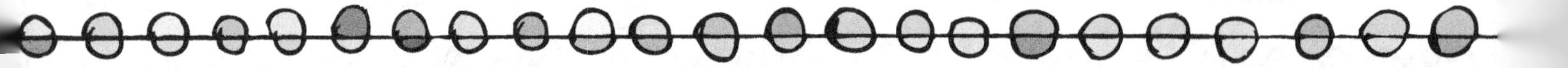

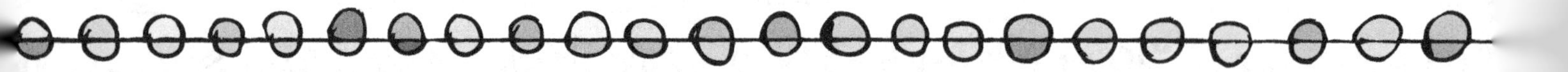